THIS JOURNAL BELONGS TO

CRUMBLE THIS PAGE

cut out this page and then crumble it
into small pieces by hand

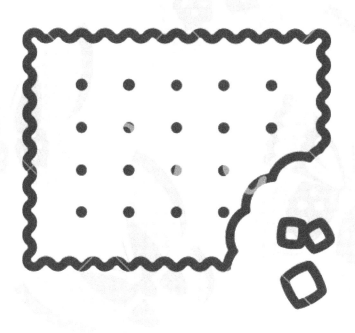

TIRE PRINT

Cut out this page, and then drive a cycle or car over it

BURN THIS PAGE

Cut out this page and then burn it using a candle - make sure you're outside the house and away from some flammable material

MAKE A PAPER PLANE

Cut out this page - make a paper plane from it and then play with it for at least 15 minutes

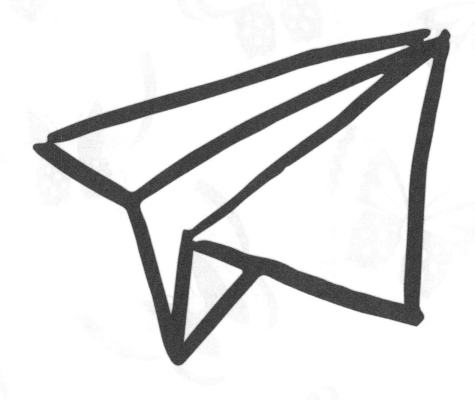

POKE SOME HOLES

Take out your pen/pencil and then poke
holes into this page

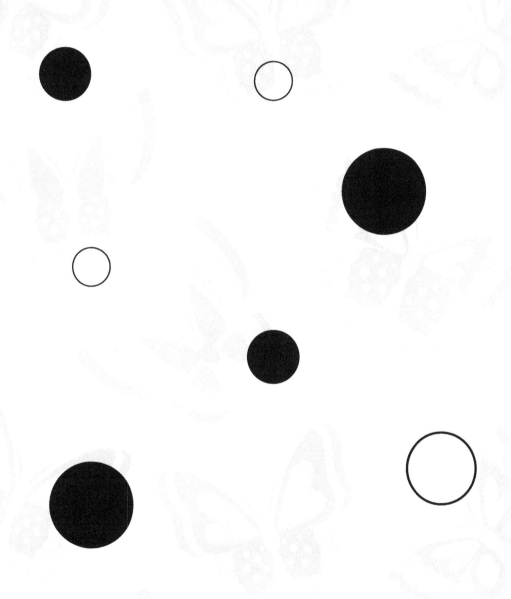

CRUSH THIS PAGE

Cut out this page and then crush it with your hands

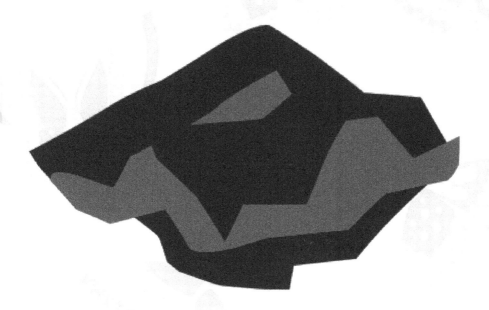

CLEAN CAR WINDOW

Cut out this page and then clean your car
window with it

CHEW THIS PAGE

Cut out this page, put it into your mouth and then chew it for some time, make sure you don't swallow it

DIP IT IN WATER

Cut out this page, dip it into a bucket of water and enjoy the scene

MAKE A BOAT

Cut out this page, make a boat with it and then throw this boat in some river

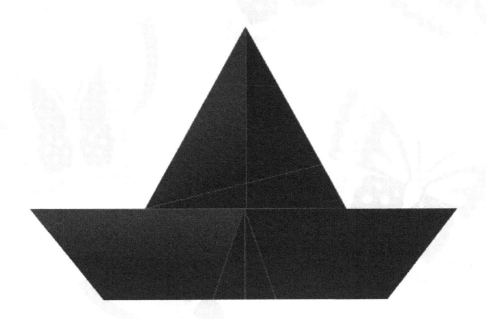

SKETCH SOME GHOSTS

Take out your pencil and start drawing a ghost picture

HAND PRINT

Color your hands and then print them on these pages

COLOR THIS PAGE

Unleash your creativity on this page

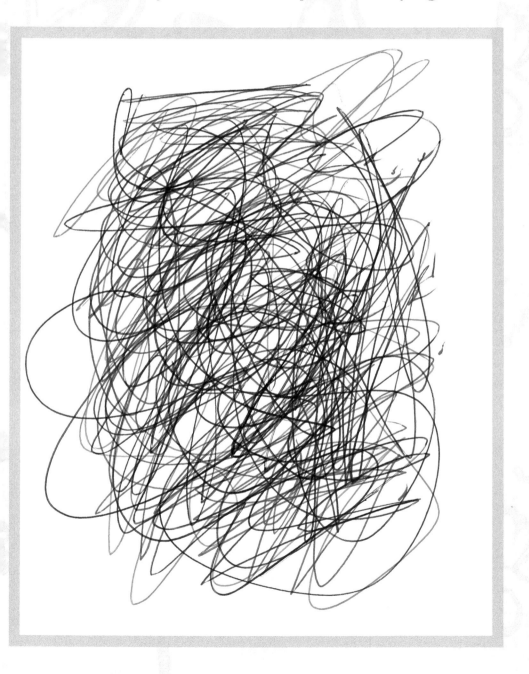

CUT OUT

Take a scissor and then cut out these figures

THROW THIS JOURNAL

Take this journal, throw it out of the window with full force and then record your experience on the next page

ADD FINGERPRINTS

Color your fingertips or use a stamp pad and then print your fingertips on this page

HIT TARGETS

Cut out this page, paste it somewhere on the wall or tree and then try to hit it with a knife (use pen if you are a below 10 yrs old) - at least 50 hits required

MAKE A BALL

Cut out the next 2 pages of this journal, make a ball from them by crushing and appying some duct tape and then play with this ball for atleast 15 minutes

THIS PAGE IS FOR MAKING A PAPER BALL

THIS PAGE IS FOR MAKING A PAPER BALL

THIS PAGE IS FOR MAKING A PAPER BALL

THIS PAGE IS FOR MAKING A PAPER BALL

THIS PAGE IS FOR MAKING A PAPER BALL

TOMATO NAME

Write you name on this page with tomato sauce

EMPTY YOUR PEN

Cut out your pen refill and then drop all of its ink on this page

DIRT SAMPLES

Collect and paste at least 5 soil samples here

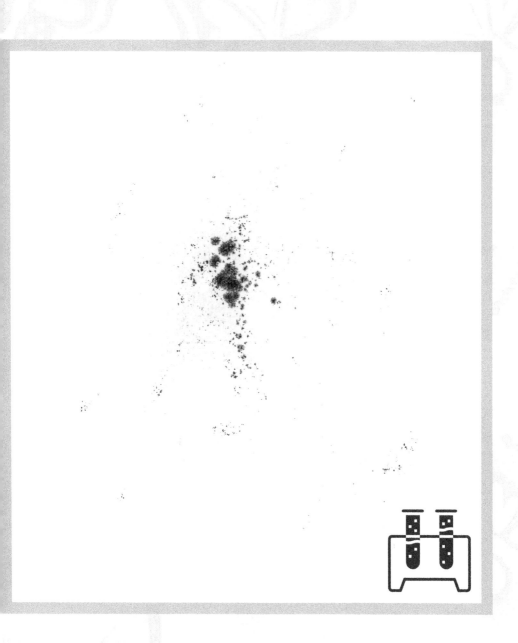

MOSQUITOES HUNT

Kill some mosquitoes and then paste them here with glue. If you don't like the idea of killing an innocent mosquito then find a dead insect and paste it here

DRAW OWN SKETCH

Take a photo and draw your own sketch

HUNG IT ON TREE

Cut out this page, hung it on tree for a whole night and then record your experience

EXPERIENCE :

BISCUIT MESS

Dip some biscuits in coffee and then drop them on this page

PUT SOME JUICE

Pour some juice on this page and then laugh out loud

NOSE PRINT

Apply some color on your nose and then print it here

KICK THIS JOURNAL

Kick this journal 4 times and then record your feelings

EXPERIENCE :

PASTE ASH

Cut and burn half of the page and then paste
its ash on another half

● ● ● ● ● ● ● ● ● ● ● ● ● ● ●

CLEAN SHOES

cut out this page and clean your shoes with it

FRY THIS PAGE

Heat some oil in frying pan and then fry this page in it (ask your parents in case of minor)

BEAT IT WITH A STICK

Beat this page with a pair of wooden sticks,
try different beats

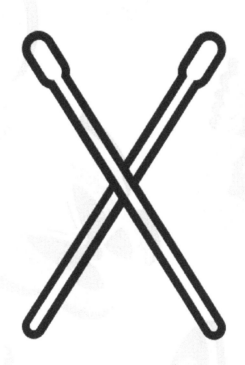

CUT ONIONS

Cut onion on this page

BRUSH THESE TEETH

Take an old toothbrush, apply some toothpaste on it and then brush these teeth

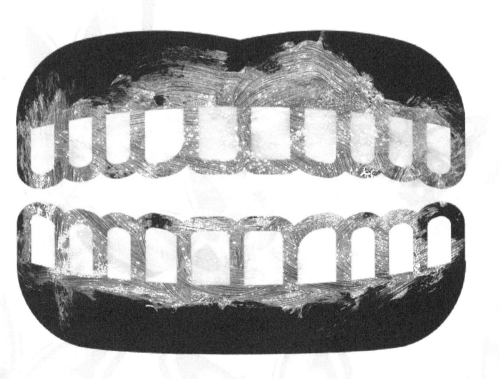

APPLY SOME MAKEUP

Make this woman look beautiful - apply some
real makeup here

RUB IT ON FLOOR

Cut out this page, rub it on floor and then record your experience

EXPERIENCE :

CUT THIS PAGE

Cut out this page, tracing the lines

SAHMPOO THESE HAIRS

Apply shampoo on these hairs with your fingertips. but first, cut out this page from the journal

BLIND WRITING

Close your eyes and then write the names of all your family members

FREEZE THIS PAGE

Cut out this page, dip it in water and then put this page in the refrigerator and let it freeze for a week

PUT BREAKFAST HERE

Take a small part of your breakfast and paste it here

MAKE SOME SNAKE

Draw some snakes here

DRY IT FOR 10 DAY

Cut out this page, dip it in water - put it on terrace and let it dry for at least 10 days

ROLL IT ON STAIRS

Roll this journal on stairs (least 3 times) and then share your experience

FLOWERS SCENT

Collect some flowers from your garden, rub them on this page to get a pleasant flower scent.

SALT AND SUGAR

Add some salt and some sugar in a cup of water and then pour it on this page

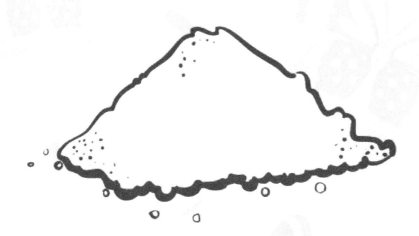

SAY THANKS

Say thanks to this journal for making your life happier

BURN THIS JOURNAL

Burn this journal or throw it in some river

Dear customers,

If you enjoyed this book, please spare a few minutes to leave us an honest review on this book's amazon product page.

Each of your review will help us to make even better products in the long run.
we're always grateful for your support and love.

PATRICIA SINGH

scan it to review this book, in just one click

Made in the USA
Monee, IL
09 December 2020